For all couples for all time.

Problems call forth
  our courage and our wisdom.

— M. SCOTT PECK

THE Twelve Gifts IN Marriage

BY CHARLENE COSTANZO

Illustrations by Paul Janovsky ◆ Photography by David Schmidt

HarperResource
An Imprint of HarperCollinsPublishers

THE TWELVE GIFTS IN MARRIAGE.

Copyright © 2005 by Charlene Costanzo.
All rights reserved. Printed in Japan.

HarperCollins books may be purchased for educational, business, or sales promotional use. For information please write: Special Markets Department, HarperCollins Publishers, Inc., 10 East 53rd Street, New York, NY 10022.

FIRST EDITION

Designed by Karen C. Heard / Chalk Design
Illustrations © 2005 by Paul Janovsky
Photography © by David Schmidt

Library of Congress Cataloging-in-Publication Data

Costanzo, Charlene.
The twelve gifts in marriage / by Charlene Costanzo ; illustrations by Paul Janovsky.
p. cm.
ISBN 0-06-074252-6
1. Marriage I. Title

HQ734C8654 2005
306.872—dc22
2004047544

05 06 07 08 09 ❖/TP 10 9 8 7 6 5 4 3 2 1

Dedicated to Frank

If we really want to love,
we must learn how to forgive.

— MOTHER TERESA

Get on with living and loving.
You don't have forever.

— LEO BUSCAGLIA

To **Mick & Donna**

From **Jeff, Sue, Nici & Megs**

Because **You ARE two very special people who have created a very special marriage. These 12 gifts can be seen both in your marriage and also in your relationships with those you love....... 25th Happy Anniversary**

Do not neglect the gift that is in you.

— 1 TIMOTHY 4:14

One day long ago a wedding took place. It began like most weddings of the time. High-spirited activity started at dawn. Customs believed to ensure compatibility, fertility, and prosperity were carefully followed. The entire village participated.

After the bride and groom exchanged promises, there was feasting and dancing.

Then it was the gift-giving time. Everyone brought something they had crafted or something they could spare, such as a candle, a blanket, a basket, or a bowl. Some brought a measure of sugar, salt, or spice. As each gift was presented, guests shouted a good wish, a bawdy tease, or a bit of practical advice.

"To happiness," someone toasted when the last gift was given.

"Today and ever after!" the crowd answered. And the feasting and dancing continued.

Late in the day an old couple arrived in the village. Passing the festivities, they headed to the inn to seek rest for the night. Observing them, the innkeeper dashed to greet them at the door. "What is the occasion?" the old woman asked.

"A wedding," panted the innkeeper. "There is still food and drink to be had. You would be welcomed. Come. Join us."

The couple paused and looked at each other. The old man touched his wife's cheek and gave her a questioning look. She smiled and nodded. And with that they turned and hastened to the village square, their eyes bright.

Finding the bride and groom, they asked to speak to them privately and took them aside. "What is it, elders?" asked the groom. "Do you bring some news for us? Where are you from?"

"We are just passing through," said the old woman.

"But we would like to offer you something," said the old man. "A caution."

The young couple stepped back.

"Please do not be afraid," said the old man. "Not a warning. Counsel,"

"Do you know what lies ahead for us?" asked the bride. "Will we live happily ever after?"

"We only know what is true for all couples," said the old woman.

"What is that?" the young woman asked.

"You will need your gifts on the journey," said the old man. "Use them every day."

The young couple was puzzled. "If we use our gifts every day, they will soon be used up or worn away," said the young woman.

"We have no journey planned. Is this a riddle?" asked the young man.

Before the old couple could answer, partyers came and carried off the bride and groom. Into the space where the young couple had stood, the old man said, "Ah, but you will travel far, even if you never leave here. Your journey will sometimes seem long. But in the end it will feel very short."

For a while the young couple found great happiness together. Both smiled often and thought, *We are blessed.*

After a time, their bliss waned. Both felt sadness but neither spoke of it. Day after day they went about their tasks with consideration. Accidental hurts were quickly forgiven. Both smiled often and thought, *We are lucky.*

As more time passed, irritations rose between them. Grudges grew. Both felt concern but neither spoke of it. Day after day they went about their rounds with resignation. Both scowled at times and thought, *We are cursed.*

One autumn day when the husband and wife shared the evening meal, silence sat with them as the sun set.

What happened to our joy? the young wife wondered.

This must be what happens with time, the husband thought. *Love fades like the light of day.*

Early the next morning the husband set out for errands in the village with thoughts of staying longer than necessary. Nearing the crossroads place, he noticed an unfamiliar figure approaching from another direction. Upon encountering the stranger, the young man remembered the mysterious couple at his wedding and recognized the old man. After exchanging greetings the young man asked about the old man's wife.

"Our journey together here has ended," sighed the old man. "She passed on."

The young man expressed sympathy.

"How is your bride?" the old man asked.

Although the young man answered that all was well, the old man read the truth in his eyes and spoke it. "So, the spell is broken," he said.

"The spell? What spell?" said the young man.

"She has become an ordinary woman and you, an ordinary man."

"Yes, we have lost something," the young man admitted.

After a moment, the old man said, "Son, first there is awe and pleasure. Then, after a time, your wondrous differences cause conflict. It may seem that love is over, but that is where it begins. Go home and learn to love."

"How?"

"Use your gifts."

"What gifts do you speak of?"

"The gifts within you," said the old man. "*Strength, Beauty, Courage, Compassion, Hope, Joy, Talent, Imagination, Reverence, Wisdom, Love,* and *Faith.*"

Reaching into his pocket, he removed a prism and handed it to the young man. "Hang this in a window that faces east or west."

"Is it magic?" asked the young man.

"No magic," said the old man. "But it may help you discover the mystery. Watch what happens when sunlight passes through it. Let the colors on your walls remind you to let light pass through you, bringing forth your gifts."

The young couple did as the old man advised and they began to understand the mystery. In every challenge they faced, they asked, "What gift can best help us now?" Always, they received an answer. In time, like the old couple, they came to realize what is true for all couples.

And, for all the rest of their days together, when rainbows danced on their walls, they danced in each other's arms and then made twelve wishes for all couples for all time.

May you look for what is good in each other.

May you respect each other's differences.

May you make time each day for moments of play.

Every day, may you be grateful.

May you show that you care when you come and go.

May you choose to love even when you feel unloving.

May you touch tenderly, speak kindly,
and listen with attention.

May you be quick to say "I am sorry"
as well as "I forgive."

May life's sorrows bring you closer together.

May troubles strengthen your commitment.

Again and again, may you renew your dreams.

And may you share your love with the world.

Living happily ever after is not the end of a fairy tale.
It is the common purpose that all life seeks.

— BOB MANDEL

AFTERWORD

*T*he *Twelve Gifts in Marriage* is based on the message of my first book, *The Twelve Gifts of Birth,* which tells of the inherent gifts we all have to help us live well. *The Twelve Gifts in Marriage* reminds us to recognize our birthright gifts and bring them into the marriage relationship.

As we use these gifts more deliberately in all our relationships and aspects of life, we discover that they are connected like the colors that emerge when light is refracted through a prism. In any situation of fear, anger, sadness, or conflict, it is helpful to ask, "Which gift can best help me now?" Personally, I am often reminded to start with hope. When I remember to trust in the goodness of life, I am led to experience yet another gift, then another, and soon the situation is transformed. Use any one of your gifts and experience the transformation. I invite you to embrace and put into practice the "twelve wishes for all couples for all time."

ACKNOWLEDGMENTS

I thank all who helped create this book, beginning with my grandparents, John and Anna Gorda, whose examples of strength, joy, and hope inspired "the old couple." Their love lives on as all love does.

In the here and now I say *thank you* to all who contribute talent toward making this world a better place, especially by bringing forth beauty. In this project: illustrator Paul Janovsky and his representative, Atelier Kimberly Boege; photographer David Schmidt, photo stylist Cindy Puskar, and photo assistant Vince Wallace; book designer Karen Heard; cover designer Andrea Brown, literary agent Ling Lucas; editor Kathryn Huck, and all colleagues at HarperCollins who participated in the making and marketing of this book.

I felt it was important to illustrate the twelve wishes with original photos of real, married couples of diverse backgrounds instead of stock shots of professional models. I thank all the Phoenix-area couples who responded to my "casting call" as well as all the individuals and organizations who helped get the word out.

And finally, to those twelve couples and the children whose schedules allowed them to work within our tight production schedule: I will treasure the memories of our photo sessions and value the responses and insights you had about the wishes which I now share with readers.

May you look for what is good in each other.
Depicted by Samantha and Jae Chang

"The wish we depicted was perfect for us, especially since we just got married. This is wisdom we can hold on to and remember when our 'honeymoon' stage is over."

May you respect each other's differences.
Depicted by Michelle and Brian Davidson

"This wish has special meaning for us. We are alike in many ways but we also have many differences that could affect the quality of our friendship and our intimacy if we let them."

May you make time each day for moments of play.

Depicted by Susan and Damon Dunn

"Sometimes it seems we never stop playing and joking. But whenever things get hectic and we haven't spent quality time together, we do 'make time for play.' A wise friend once told us that a marriage does not last based on how much you love each other but rather how many times you forgive each other."

Every day, may you be grateful.

Depicted by Gada and Juhdi Jasser

"All that is good comes from God," they say. "To be grateful is to believe in God,"

May you show that you care when you come and go.

Depicted by Heather and Tad Smith

"It's the little choices made every day that make or break a marriage. After twelve years of marriage, we don't tell each other 'I love you' every day with words, but we show it with mutual kindness and respect."

May you choose to love even when you feel unloving.

Depicted by Veronica and Dustin Jones

"Having met and started dating during our late teen years, we've grown into adulthood and learned a lot together. Learning to love through all the ups and downs is a powerful force that has fused our souls for all time."

May you touch tenderly, speak kindly, and listen with attention.

Depicted by Michelle and Cameron Bolender

"Treating each other with care breeds love and helps avoid many hurts. When conflicts do happen, we never go to bed angry. Even if it takes all night, we talk until we work it out."

May you be quick to say "I'm sorry" as well as "I forgive."

Depicted by Miriam and Joe Palmer

"It is ironic we were blessed with portraying this wish. It is the one that speaks the most to us right now. Joe is very forgiving and quick to say 'I'm sorry,' but for me, it is more of a challenge. It takes me longer to let go and release disappointment and resentment and get to that place of understanding, forgiveness, and peace," Miriam says.

May life's sorrows bring you closer together.

Depicted by Judy and Jim Banyai

The Banyais are high school sweethearts married since 1961. For them, the most important wish to live by is *Every day, may you be grateful*. "In a mind-set of gratitude all challenges are met, all joys appreciated, and all love expressed," they say.

May troubles strengthen your commitment.

Depicted by Sandy and Larry James

Larry is the author of several relationship enrichment books, including *How to Really Love the One You're With*. In fact, the quotes opening and closing *The Twelve Gifts in Marriage* were cited from that book. Larry and Sandy also feel that *Every day, may you be grateful* is the most powerful wish. "Sandy lost a daughter and her first husband some years ago. The anniversary of their passing is a time for both of us to reflect upon how precious life is."

Again and again, may you renew your dreams.

Depicted by Sylvia and Gene Richardson

"Our biggest dream is, and was from the beginning, to be each other's safe place. We have a deep and abiding trust in each other. We renew this dream consistently. We are accessible to each other even when the rest of the world seems frighteningly shaky."

And may you share your love with the world.

Depicted by Trish and Paul Howey

"All these wishes are important in a loving relationship. In fact, they seem to be inextricably connected. But we think gratitude is paramount and we are sure to express it every day."

Appearing with the Howeys in this photo is their dog, Freckles, along with Alexander Maschoff, Malik Bullok, and Gabrielle Ortiz. This scene depicts the way the Howeys share their love with the world by sharing Freckles with youngsters as a reminder to love and respect one another and all living things. The Howeys adopted Freckles, who had been abandoned in the Arizona desert. They recognized her extraordinary gentleness and trained her to become a certified therapy dog. Together, they visit schools and shelters where many of the children come from backgrounds of abuse and homelessness. For more about this story, read *Freckles: The Mystery of the Little White Dog in the Desert*.

I acknowledge programs that enrich marriages and help hurting ones heal, especially Marriage Encounter and Retrouvaille, and all the couples who share their love with the world by coordinating such programs. It was at a Marriage Encounter program in the 1970s that my husband, Frank, and I first heard the expression and began to understand that "love is a decision."

Finally, I thank my family and friends for their ongoing love and encouragement. A special thank you to Frank for helping me give birth to this book and for continuing to discover the mysteries of love with me as we share a path on this journey.

*Let the winds of the heavens
dance between you.*

— KAHLIL GIBRAN

Please visit
www.**The Twelve Gifts**.com

To learn more about
The Twelve Gifts

or to contact
Charlene Costanzo

Let all that you do be done in love.

— 1 CORINTHIANS 16: 13–14